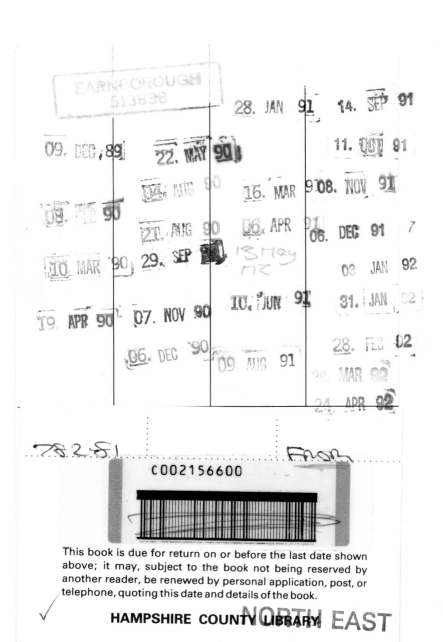

From Broadway To Piccadilly.

Curtain Raisers.

Wise Publications.
London/New York/Sydney

Exclusive distributors:
Music Sales Limited,
8/9 Frith Street,
London W1V 5TZ,
England.
Music Sales Pty Limited,
120 Rothschild Street,
Rosebery, NSW 2018,
Australia.

This book © Copyright 1988 by
Wise Publications.
UK ISBN 0.7119.1423.0
Order No. AM70186

Designed by Pearce Marchbank Studio.
Compiled by Peter Evans.

Music Sales' complete catalogue lists thousands of
titles and is free from your local music shop, or direct from
Music Sales Limited. Please send £1 in stamps for postage to
Music Sales Limited, 8/9 Frith Street, London W1V 5TZ.

Printed in the United Kingdom by
Anchor Brendon Limited, Tiptree, Essex.

Oh, What A Beautiful Mornin'

Words by Oscar Hammerstein II
Music by Richard Rodgers

5

Do-Re-Mi

Words by Oscar Hammerstein II
Music by Richard Rodgers

What Kind Of Fool Am I

Words & Music by Leslie Bricusse & Anthony Newley

14

Tonight

Music by Leonard Bernstein
Lyrics by Stephen Sondheim

slow - ly And still the sky is light. _____ O

moon, grow bright, And make this end - less day end - less

night _____ to - night! _____ to -

night! _____

Edelweiss

Words by Oscar Hammerstein II
Music by Richard Rodgers

I Dreamed A Dream (From The Musical 'Les Misérables')

Music by Claude-Michel Schonberg
Lyrics by Herbert Kretzmer
Original Text by Alain Boublil & Jean-Marc Natel

Till There Was You

Words & Music by Meredith Willson

Sit Down, You're Rocking The Boat

Words & Music by Frank Loesser

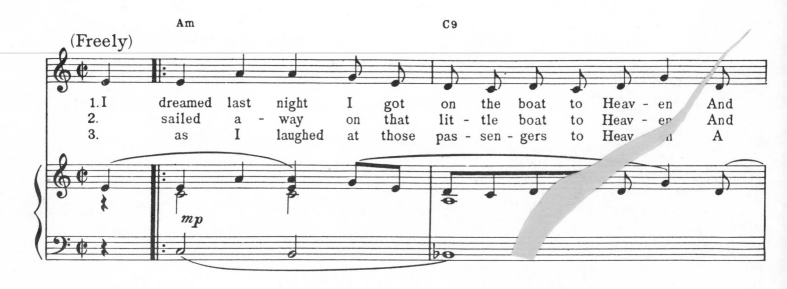

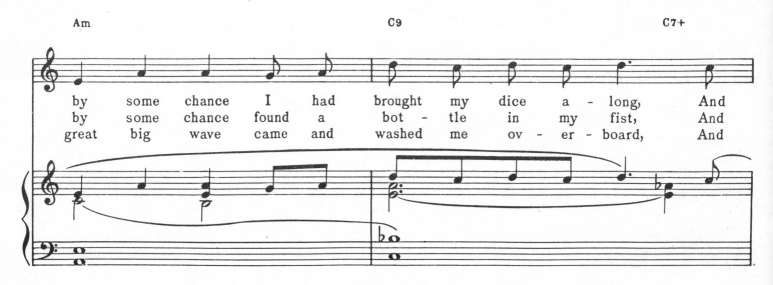

there I stood and I hol - lered, "Some - one fade me", But the
there I I stood nice - ly pas - sin' out the whis - key, But the
as I sank, and I hol - lered, "Some - one save me"; That's the

pas - sen - gers they knew right from wrong For the
pas - sen - gers were bound to re - sist For the
mo - ment I woke up, to thank the Lord And I

religioso
a tempo

Chorus with a beat

peo - ple all said, "Sit down,__ sit down__ you're rock - in' the
peo - ple all said, "Be - ware __ you're on __ a heav - en - ly
said to my - self, "Sit down __ sit down __ you're rock - in' the

mf

boat." Peo - ple all said, "Sit down__ sit down____
trip." Peo - ple all said, "Be - ware__ be - ware____
boat." Said to my - self, "Sit down__ sit down____

Day by Day

Words & Music by Stephen Schwartz

31

The Ugly Duckling

Words & Music by Frank Loesser

went with a quack and a wad-dle and a quack in a flur-ry of Ei-der-down.

That poor lit-tle ug-ly duck-ling went wan-der-ing far and near but at ev-'ry place they said to his face now ✺✶! get out of here ✺✶! get out, ✺✶!

get out get out get out of here. And he went with a quack and a

wad-dle and a quack and a ver-y un-hap-py tear.

All thru the win-ter-time he hid him-self a-

way. A-shamed to show his face. A-fraid of what oth-ers might

say. All thru the win-ter in his lone-ly clump of

weed 'Til a flock of swans spied him there and ver-y soon a-

GACEb

greed "You're a ver-y fine swan in - deed!" *(Spoken:)* "Swan? me a

swan? Aw go on!" "You're a swan! Take a look at your-self in the

As Time Goes By

Words & Music by Herman Hupfeld

Moon-light and love songs nev-er out of date, Hearts full of pas - sion, jeal-ous-y and hate;

mf-f *poco a poco cresc:*

Wo-man needs man and man must have his mate, That no one can de - ny. It's

poco rit.

p-mf

still the same old sto-ry, a fight for love and glo-ry, A case of do or die! The

a tempo

world will al-ways wel-come lov-ers, as time goes by. You by.

41

Big D

Words & Music by Frank Loesser

44

Somewhere

Music by Leonard Bernstein
Lyrics by Stephen Sondheim

Tomorrow

Music by Charles Strouse
Words by Martin Charnin

The sun'll come out__ to-mor-row, bet your bot-tom dol-lar that to- mor-row__ there'll be sun! Jus'

think-ing a-bout___ to-mor-row clears a-way the cob-webs and the sor-row__ 'til there's none. When I'm stuck_with a

day that's gray and lone-ly, I just stick_out my chin and grin and say:_____

Luck Be A Lady

Words & Music by Frank Loesser

50

Lady with me. _____ A
lady does-n't leave her es-cort_____ It is-n't
fair _____ It is-n't nice! _____ A
lady does-n't wan-der all ov-er the room and
blow on some oth-er guy's dice. _____ So,

Younger Than Springtime

Words by Oscar Hammerstein II
Music by Richard Rodgers

are you, An-gel and lov-er, heav-en and earth are you to me. And when your youth and joy in-vade my arms And fill my heart as now they do...

America

Music by Leonard Bernstein
Lyrics by Stephen Sondheim

Verse

Girl: 1. I like the ci-ty of San Juan.___ Boy: I know a boat you can
Girl: 2. I'll drive a Bu-ick through San Juan.___ Boy: If there's a road you can
Girl: 3. When I will go back to San Juan.___ Boy: When you will shut up and
Girl: 4. I'll bring a T. V. to San Juan.___ Boy: If there's a cur-rent to

get on.___ Girl: Hund-reds of flow-ers in
drive on.___ Girl: I'll give my cous-ins a
get gone?___ Girl: I'll give them new wash-ing
turn on.___ Girl: Ev-'ry-one there will give

8va ad lib.

full bloom.___ Boy: Hund-reds of peo-ple in each room!___
free ride.___ Boy: How you fit all of them in-side?___
ma-chine.___ Boy: What have they got there to keep clean?___
big cheer.___ Boy: Ev-'ry-one there will have moved here!___

(sing octave lower ad lib.)

I'll Never Fall In Love Again

Words by Hal David
Music by Burt Bacharach

I'll nev - er fall in love a - gain.

Don't tell me what it's all a - bout, 'Cause I've been there and I'm

glad I'm out; Out of those chains, those chains that bind you, That is why I'm

here to re - mind you.
here to re - mind you. What do you get when you fall in love, You

Diamonds Are A Girl's Best Friend

Words by Leo Robin
Music by Jule Styne

Gm7 C7   F

pen - sive   jew - els; _____
keep their   flick - er; _____

a tempo

Chorus
C7   F   B♭ F   C7

A   kiss   on   the   hand   may   be   quite   Con - ti - nen - tal   But
There   may   come   a   time   when   a   lass   needs   a   law - yer,   But

F   Fdim   Gm6   C9♭   C7   D7   Gm

Dia - monds Are A   Girl's   Best   Friend, _____   A   kiss   may   be
Dia - monds Are A   Girl's   Best   Friend, _____   There   may   come   a

D7   G   Am7 Gdim   G   Am7 G7

grand   But   it   won't   pay   the   rent - al   on   your   hum - ble   flat ——   Or
time   When   a   hard   boiled   em - ploy - er   thinks   you're   aw   ful   nice, ——   But

65

Maybe This Time

Music by John Kander
Lyrics by Fred Ebb

If My Friends Could See Me Now

Words by Dorothy Fields
Music by Cy Coleman

My Kind Of Girl

Words & Music by Leslie Bricusse

Cabaret

Music by John Kander
Lyrics by Fred Ebb

Seventy Six Trombones

Words & Music by Meredith Willson

Big Spender

Words by Dorothy Fields
Music by Cy Coleman

I don't pop my cork for ev'-ry guy I see.

Hey! Big Spen-der,_____ Spend a lit-tle time___with

me. Would-n't you like to have

fun, fun, fun? How's a-bout a few laughs, laughs? I can show you a

Send In The Clowns

Words & Music by Stephen Sondheim

Something's Coming

Music by Leonard Bernstein
Lyrics by Stephen Sondheim

to me.

Will it be?___ Yes, it will.___ May-be just___ by

hold-ing still___ It 'll be there.___

95

I Know Him So Well

Words & Music by Benny Andersson, Tim Rice & Bjorn Ulvaeus

1. No-thing is so good it lasts e - ter-nal-ly,———— per-fect si - tu-a-tions must go wrong.
2. Look-ing back I could have played it dif-ferent-ly,———— won a few more moments, who can tell.

But this has nev-er yet pre-vent-ed me _____
But it took time to un-der-stand the man. _____

want-ing far too much for far too long.
Now at least I know I know him well. Was-n't it good?

Oh, so good! _____ Oh, so fine! _____ He can't be mine?

Was-n't he fine? _____ Is-n't it mad-ness he can't be mine?

But in the end he needs a lit-tle bit more than me, more se-

He needs his fan-ta-sy and free-dom.

-cu-ri-ty.

I know him so well.

No-one in your life is with you con-stant-ly, no-one is com-plete-ly on your

Look-ing back I could have played it dif-fer-ent-ly, learned a-bout the man be-fore I

5

(tacet 1:st x) Look-ing back I could have played things some oth-er way.

mf

101

Nothing

Words by Edward Kleban
Music by Marvin Hamlisch

I'm so excited because I'm gonna go to the High School of Performing Arts.
I mean, I was dying to be a serious actress. Anyway it's the first day
of acting class and we're in the auditorium and the teacher, Mister Karp,
puts us up on the stage with our legs around everybody, one in back of
the other, and he says: O.K., we're gonna do improvisations. Now, you're
on a bobsled and it's snowing out and it's cold. O.K., go!

104

Climb Ev'ry Mountain

Words by Oscar Hammerstein II
Music by Richard Rodgers

4030

The Joint Is Jumpin'

Words by Andy Razaf & J C Johnson
Music by Thomas Waller

Don't Cry For Me Argentina

Music by Andrew Lloyd Webber
Lyrics by Tim Rice

Slowly
INTRODUCTION

(quasi harp)

1. It won't be ea-sy, you'll think it strange   When I

try to ex-plain how I feel, That I still need your love af-ter all that I've done:___

___ You won't be-lieve me All you will see is a girl you once knew Al-

though she's dressed up to the nines at six-es and sev-ens with you.

VERSE

2. I had to let it hap-pen, I had to change; Could-n't stay all my life down at heel: Look-ing

Horns

out of the win-dow, stay-ing out of the sun. So I chose free - dom

Run-ning a-round try-ing ev-'ry-thing new, but no-thing im-pressed me at all, I

nev-er ex-pect-ed it to. Don't cry for me Ar-gen - ti - na _____ the

truth is I nev - er left you: All through my wild days, my mad ex - ist-ence, I kept my

I Don't Know How To Love Him

Music by Andrew Lloyd Webber
Lyrics by Tim Rice

Slowly, tenderly and very expressively

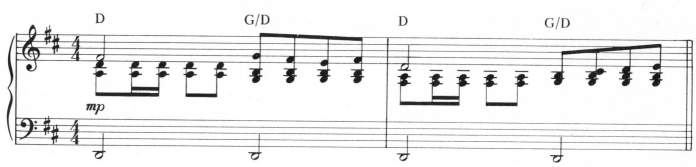

Underneath The Arches

Words & Music by Bud Flanagan